"The apostle Paul tells Christians we are made to follow Jesus together! The church is not a Sunday morning gathering, it is a whole way of life. The days of sitting in pews pointing in the same direction one day a week as 'church' are melting away. But how do we do that? Fitch gives us direction for taking the next step."

—**BRUXY CAVEY,** pastor of The Meeting House and author of *Reunion* and *The End of Religion*

"When many are asking why bother when it comes to church, Fitch draws from the heart of the Anabaptist tradition to present a refreshing vision of a gathered community focused on Jesus, enjoying divine fellowship, and expressing faith in biblical practices, edifying habits, and acts of justice and love. If you (or people you know) have lost hope, spend an hour with Fitch."

—**NIJAY K. GUPTA,** professor of New Testament at Northern Seminary

"David Fitch presents a compelling vision of the church as a community of practices tending to the presence of Christ in the world. At a time when both the credibility and coherence of church is in doubt, this book is a hopeful and inspiring return to the biblical basics—a welcome message for Christian leaders navigating mission in a post-Christendom world."

—**EMILY MCGOWIN,** assistant professor of theology at Wheaton College

"David Fitch's theological treatise *What Is the Church?* reinvigorates imagination for what the church needs to be in these apocalyptic times. Church isn't simply a service on Sunday morning but a joyful, healing, loving, faithful, surprised-filled community that bears witness to the politics of Jesus, offering his presence and life to the world."

—**JR WOODWARD,** national director of the V3 Movement, author of *Creating a Missional Culture,* and co-author of *The Church as Movement*

"David Fitch gives us hope that church still matters. *What Is the Church?* gives a biblical, historical, and practical picture of how the church is meant to be an instrument of God's transformative work in the world. Fitch's analysis can invigorate those who might be discouraged over the church's current ambiguous place in society."

—**DENNIS EDWARDS,** author of *Might from the Margins* and associate professor of New Testament at North Park Seminary

"David Fitch offers an account of the church different than the account of hegemonic Western Christendom. Indeed, he takes us back to the ways of Jesus, where church is defined by the communion of practices, culture of presence, and sense of mission. A must read for anyone keen on seeing the church renewed in its mission as God's mode of presence."

—**MABIALA KENZO,** professor of theology at Faculté de Théologie Evangélique de Boma and director of District Saint-Laurent, Alliance Chretienne et Missionnaire au Quebec

# What Is the Church

*and Why Does It Exist?*

THE JESUS WAY
—SMALL BOOKS *of* RADICAL FAITH—

# What Is the Church

*and Why Does*

*It Exist?*

DAVID E. FITCH

HERALD
PRESS

Harrisonburg, Virginia

Herald Press
PO Box 866, Harrisonburg, Virginia 22803
www.HeraldPress.com

WHAT IS THE CHURCH AND WHY DOES IT EXIST?
© 2021 by Herald Press, Harrisonburg, Virginia 22803. 800-245-7894.
    All rights reserved.
Library of Congress Control Number: 2020951003
International Standard Book Number: 978-1-5138-0570-2 (paper)
    978-1-5138-0619-8 (ebook)
Printed in United States of America

Unless otherwise noted, Scripture text is quoted, with permission, from the *New Revised Standard Version*, © 1989, Division of Christian Education of the National Council of Churches of Christ in the United States of America.

25 24 23 22 21          11 10 9 8 7 6 5 4 3 2

# Contents

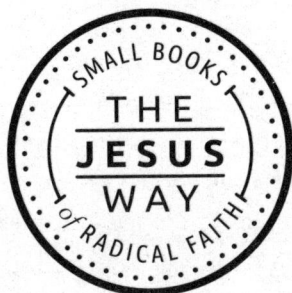

# Introduction to The Jesus Way Series from Herald Press

The Jesus Way is good news for all people, of all times, in all places. Jesus Christ "is before all things, and in him all things hold together"; "in him all the fullness of God was pleased to dwell" (Colossians 1:17, 19). The Jesus Way happens when God's will is done on earth as it is in heaven.

But what does it mean to walk the Jesus Way? How can we who claim the name of Christ reflect the image of God in the twenty-first century? What does it mean to live out and proclaim the good news of reconciliation in Christ?

The Jesus Way: Small Books of Radical Faith offers concise, practical theology that helps readers encounter big questions about God's work in the world. Grounded in a Christ-centered reading of Scripture and a commitment to reconciliation, the series aims to enliven the service and embolden the witness of people who follow Jesus. The volumes in the series are written by a diverse community of internationally renowned pastors, scholars, and practitioners committed to the way of Jesus.

The Jesus Way series is rooted in Anabaptism, a Christian tradition that prioritizes following Jesus, loving enemies, and creating faithful communities. During the Protestant Reformation of the 1500s, early Anabaptists who began meeting for worship emphasized discipleship in addition to belief, baptized adults instead of infants, and pledged their allegiance to God over loyalty to the state. Early Anabaptists were martyred for their radical faith, and they went to their deaths without violently resisting their accusers.

Today more than two million Anabaptist Christians worship in more than one hundred countries around the globe. They include Mennonites, Amish, Brethren in Christ, and Hutterites. Many other Christians committed to Anabaptist beliefs and practices remain in church communities in other traditions.

Following Jesus means turning from sin, renouncing violence, seeking justice, believing in the reconciling power of God, and living in the power of the Holy Spirit. The Jesus Way liberates us from conformity to the world and heals broken places. It shines light on evil and restores all things.

Join Christ-followers around the world as we seek the Jesus Way.

# Introduction

These are tumultuous times to be a Christian in the West. Many of our churches are aging, shrinking, or just plain dying. Some of the largest and most visible churches in North America have imploded before our very eyes as their once-revered leaders have committed moral failures of monstrous proportions. The epidemic of sexual abuse perpetrated by pastors and priests of the Southern Baptist and Roman Catholic churches, among others, has left all of us shaking our heads. We're left asking whether anything good can come from the organized church.

Recently, political protests have erupted across the country in response to police violence against Black men and women. Overnight, hundreds of thousands of people have mobilized to protest the racist systems of power that allow such injustices to continue unchecked. The church, meanwhile, seems invisible. For those who are passionate for the work of justice in the world, the church seems impotent, incapable of contributing in any meaningful way.

On top of this, the alignment of many evangelical churches in the United States with the Trump administration, and its seeming disregard toward those harmed by the injustices of racism, socioeconomic inequities, and exclusionary immigration policies, has added immensely to the cultural cynicism toward the church in North America. Many Christians of the millennial generation and younger, raised as children in these churches, now question the relevance of the church. The church, it seems, has abused its power one too many times to be given another chance. As a result, many Christians today are asking, "Who needs the church?" We seem to be experiencing nothing less than the collapse of the modern church in the West.

When things get chaotic, and no longer seem to make sense, we must go back to the "what" and the "why" questions. We must ask all over again: What are we doing here when we gather as the church and why are we doing it? Only then can we get to the "how" question. Only then can we discern how to be faithful to who we are and the mission we have been given.

Perhaps this is a cultural moment that offers us an opportunity to reset the church in North America. Perhaps this is an ideal time for Christians everywhere to reexamine what it means to be the church. It is an occasion for us to ask all over again what we are doing here, who we are, and how we should live as a part of the local church.

Historically, Anabaptist churches have faced situations similar to the ones Christians now confront in North America. Christians find themselves today in disfavor within the culture: no longer respected, even resented, and having lost cultural power. Anabaptists have not only been here before, they have asked whether these exact cultural situations might help us shape the right way to be the church.

Anabaptists first arose during the Protestant Reformation in Europe as a movement of Christians who resisted alignment of the church with the state and other powerful cultural institutions. In the midst of the Reformation, Anabaptists were a persecuted minority, renounced even by the so-called Reformers. Many Anabaptists rejected the worldly authority of "the sword"—any use of official force—rejecting the power of government, the military, national legislation, and other kinds of coercive control. They believed that God was at work powerfully—just not through coercion, violence, or force. The church, they said, should be a witness to who God is, what God is doing, and how God is transforming the world through Jesus Christ. This is best done by following Jesus and living as a people under his reign. The church should live as citizens of the kingdom of God, whose ruler came to be with people rather than to use power over them and against them.

These historical Anabaptists, and the wisdom gained by their successors, can offer much help for us today in thinking through how to live as the church in a time when we have lost cultural power and influence. They can help us ask all-important questions for the times we live in: What is church? Why is it so important? And how do we live as the church in our own time and place?

This book is an attempt to answer these questions as concisely as possible. In chapters 1 and 2, I unpack the simple question "What is the church?" What defines the church? How is a church different from other social organizations? In chapters 3 and 4, I move to the question "Why the church?" Is it necessary for Christians to be part of a church? Why does God even need the church to accomplish a mission of bringing justice and salvation in the world? In chapters 5 and 6, after navigating the *what*, and the inescapable fact that the church is indispensable to who we are as Christians and God's mission in the world, I offer some reflections on how the church should live. Given the nature of the church and a conviction that the church is indispensable, what should our life together look like? It is my hope that, perhaps, through this short book, God can use these reflections to kindle a conversation about who we are as the church. And I hope God can stir a reimagining of the church by the Spirit to meet the challenges we face in these most challenging of times.

# 1

# What Is the Church? A Practicing Community

What is the church? Is it a group of people who happen to believe in the same things? Is it a club that people join for membership benefits? Is it a political party that organizes people to work together to achieve a common cause? What holds the people of the church together? And what brings us together in the first place?

There are multiple answers to these questions, but perhaps the best place to start is by saying this: The church is a community of practices that join people together in their submission to Jesus as Lord. **Practices** are exercises people do together that work in some way to achieve a common purpose. (Key terms appear in bold and are defined in the glossary.) When Christians join together in practices as given by Jesus Christ, the result is a common way of life made possible in his life, death, resurrection, and ascension. This way of life in turn

witnesses to the world what God has done and is doing to
reconcile the whole world to himself.

This is the way the New Testament describes the church.
For example, Acts 2:41-42 paints a picture of a group of people "who received [Peter's] word" about Jesus, and then came
together around a set of practices. These included baptism,
devotion to the apostles' teaching, fellowship, the breaking
of bread, and prayer. These people became the first church.
According to this description, the church is a people gathered
in allegiance to Christ and committed to a common set of
practices that define their life together.

Likewise, the apostle Paul in 1 Corinthians 12 describes the
church at Corinth as "the body" of Christ, formed through the
participation of all its members in the gifts of the Holy Spirit.
Jesus Christ is the center, and it is through the practicing of
these gifts that a people is formed into a social group where
Christ's very presence and authority are made manifest. The
apostle Peter (1 Peter 2:9) describes several early congrega-
tions as "a people" chosen by God to be God's very own and
to live in a specific way so that "you may proclaim the mighty
acts of him who called you out of darkness into his marvelous
light" (NRSV). Jesus is the revelation of God that results in
this gathered community (1 Peter 1:7). The descriptors "royal
priesthood" and "holy nation" accentuate that this community has a distinctive way of life in the world. For the New
Testament then, the church is a distinctive way of life, defined
by common practices, centered in a relationship to the Lordship of Jesus.

The Greek term **ekklesia** is used frequently in the New Testament to describe the church. Paul uses it forty-nine times,
more than any other term, to address local churches in his
letters. The writer of Acts uses it twenty-three times to describe

the emerging groups of people gathering to worship Jesus in the first decades after Christ's resurrection. In the Greco-Roman culture of the day, *ekklesia* was used most often to describe civic assemblies that met in each city to determine the laws and policies.[1] Citizens of each city would meet to practice open discussion, discernment, and to legislate guidance on issues of local civic importance.[2] The New Testament writers, by labeling the local churches *ekklesia*, suggest that these churches were social bodies responsible for doing similar kinds of practices. Except, in contrast to civic assemblies, the churches of Jesus Christ gathered to discern how best to live under the rule of a different authority, the authority of Jesus as Lord.

From all appearances, the New Testament church began as a people gathered by a common allegiance to Jesus as Lord, living lives characterized by practices that shaped them into a common way of life made possible in him. Perhaps we too should begin new churches, or the renewal of existing ones, in the same way, by centering a people in Jesus Christ through a set of practices that reflect our allegiance to Jesus.

## THEN CAME THE CREEDS

Interestingly, a shift in understanding church identity began around 313 AD. Constantine, a convert to Christianity and the Emperor of Rome, signed the Edict of Milan, a decree that provided government protections for Christians and their churches within the Roman Empire. Previously Christians had been persecuted but now, in some ways at least, Christians became favored in the culture.

In 325 AD, in response to doctrinal disagreements (over who Jesus is), Constantine convened the first ecumenical council, calling over two hundred bishops from every church in the Roman Empire to the city of Nicaea to resolve the disagreement. A creed was written and approved. This creed was later amended and refined in the city of Constantinople in 381 AD, where it became orthodoxy for the church universal. The creed is still known around the world as the **Nicene Creed**.

This Council of Nicaea centralized a new authority for the church worldwide. The Nicene Creed was assumed as authoritative for all churches of Jesus Christ everywhere. It was organized around three articles, headed by the Father, Son, and Holy Spirit. Each was written in the form of a confession, beginning with the words "We believe."[3] At the Council of Constantinople, the third article was expanded to include a statement about the church, saying, "We believe in one, holy, catholic, and apostolic Church." With the adoption of this creed, the Christian understanding of the church shifted. The church gets conceptualized; we go from the church as something we do together to the church as something we believe in. And it changes significantly how we think about what we call church.

We can see the impact of this development by examining each one of the creedal adjectives that describes the church: one, holy, catholic, apostolic.

For instance, in the Nicene Creed, *one* refers to the unity of the church, something Jesus prayed for in John 17:21. As part of this unity, Jesus called every Christian to the practice of reconciliation within the church. With each conflict, grievance, or sin against someone, Jesus called those who follow him to practice listening, confessing, submitting one to another, discerning, reconciling, and healing (Matthew 18:15-20; James 5:16). Reconciliation is something we do that we call church.

But when we say, "We believe in the *one* church," something shifts. There is a sense that unity becomes something we believe in as opposed to a practice of reconciliation we commit to in the work of living our life together under the authority of Jesus. There's a danger in this shift, in that unity now becomes something to be enforced from the top down as opposed to something worked out among a group of people under the authority of Jesus. Imagine a member (or a priest) of a fourth-century church declaring one Sunday that they no longer believe "Jesus is God in the Greek sense of the word *homousian*" (the word used in the Nicene creed meaning "same essence"). They now are questioned by the authorities. They are judged to be a heretic according to the Nicene Creed and kicked out of the church. Instead of discerning together what this actual disagreement is about, heresy becomes a thing to be enforced in the post-**Constantinian** West. This is an over-simplification, but such an episode illustrates how the subtle changes surrounding the creeds can change the nature of how we think about church.

Theologian Ephraim Radner has proposed that we should not see unity as an ideal of perfect harmony in all relations that churches somehow reach. Instead the church by nature is always in process of sorting out its disagreements. This sorting is part of a way of life. In fact, it is our conflicts and the way we practice reconciliation in the midst of them that gives witness to our unity in Christ. That is how unity in Christ works. Radner calls this "A Brutal Unity."[4] And so it is in the practice of reconciliation together amid disagreements that unity in Christ manifests itself.[5]

The second term, *holy*, describes the church's distinctive way of life, its "set-apartness." Jesus prayed that God would "sanctify them in the truth" in John 17:17. He expected the church would grow in holiness through relationship to him, his reign, and his way. The word *holy* is about the church's practice of discipleship, of daily growing in Christ. But once again by saying "We believe" in the holy church, a subtle change becomes noticeable. As opposed to understanding holiness as something we do, it becomes an ideal in which we believe.

The danger now is that holiness becomes something to be enforced on people from a position of authority rather than something worked out (practiced) over time in a community. We've seen this happen repeatedly in the church's history. For instance, famously, Donatus, a bishop in North Africa in the fourth century, refused to honor the authority of priests who had fallen from the faith during the Diocletian persecutions. His followers, the Donatists, argued that priests who had fallen from the faith during the persecution and had denied Christ could no longer be priests or preside over the **sacraments** unless they were restored, rebaptized, and re-ordained to their faith. The Donatists claimed that any sacraments presided over by a fallen priest with such unholy character would be ineffectual. Ironically, just a few years after he became the emperor, Constantine (and later Augustine) sided against the Donatists in this conflict. They were declared heretics and troops were sent in to confiscate church properties. For both sides of the conflict, then, their own version of holiness became a standard to be enforced on the church. This is not incidental. This kind of coercion is what happens when holiness becomes a concept we believe in instead of a practice to be lived out.

Early in the last century rampant alcoholism was destroying many lives, marriages, and families in North America. Certain churches within the holiness movement discerned among themselves that alcohol was an instrument of evil, aligned with demonic forces. The discernment in these churches was that all should abstain from alcohol for the good of each other. This led to the temperance movement and even to the prohibition of alcohol nationwide. As a result, many lives were saved, many families and marriages preserved. The Holy Spirit worked for the sanctification of many Christians during this time.

Seventy-five years later, however, something had changed in some holiness churches. The discernment around "no drinking" had become extracted from the daily practice of discipleship and instead became a belief to enforce. In certain holiness denominations, clergy were required to sign teetotalism clauses and were disciplined if caught with an alcoholic drink. "No drinking" now defined what it meant to "come out from among them, and be ye separate" (2 Corinthians 6:17 KJV). The issue even divided those who considered themselves good holiness Christians from those who were deemed to be not serious about their Christian walk. Along the way, the church lost the very process of discernment in the Spirit that originally led the church to discern those things in the first place. Instead the church got defined by a rule: we are the church "who doesn't drink!"

Whenever holiness becomes extracted from the believer's everyday life of discipleship and becomes a test of every believer's faith, bad things happen. Holiness becomes something to believe in rather than something worked out in our daily lives. It becomes coercive, not enlivening, life-giving, and transformative.[6] Things like sexuality, marriage and divorce, money, and addiction become areas of shaming instead of opportunities for faith, submission, obedience, discernment, healing, and Spirit empowerment in God's presence. We lose the very practices that shape our way of life. And it is questionable whether what is left can still be considered "church."

The third term, *catholic*, describes the church as universal. (Note this different meaning from the capitalized *Catholic*,

which means Roman Catholic.) In other words, it acknowl-
edges that all churches everywhere are connected because,
after all, we all worship the same Christ. As the writer of
Colossians 1:17-18 proclaims, "He is before all things, and
in him all things hold together . . . He is the head of the body,
the church." This is a unique bond among all the churches in
the world: we together are the church universal. It is such a
beautiful idea.

This statement about the catholic nature of the church was
uncontroversial, in the West at least, over several hundred
years after the Council of Constantinople. Then the Reformation came, and the church divided in Europe between those
who followed Luther, Calvin, or remained Roman Catholic.
Roman Catholics claimed that the Reformers were not the real
church and, in essence, excommunicated the Reformers. The
Reformers rejected this judgment, and Luther called the pope
(the ultimate authority in Rome) the antichrist. Both Catholics
and Protestants were left with the question: What (or who) is
the real church?

The Reformers solved the problem by asserting that not
everybody within the church is Christian, i.e., part of the true
church. Instead, the true church is invisible with its membership known only to God. This invisible true church resides
inside the visible church. The church as gathered is now a
mixture of true Christians and those who are not Christian.
Ultimately, since the true church is now invisible, the true
church becomes an article of faith rather than a visible reality
Christians participate in through practices.

Once again, "church" becomes a concept to believe in
as opposed to something we do together. And because we
now assume that wherever the concrete church meets it will
always be a mixture of true Christians and non-Christians,

we will assume there are hypocrites among us who are not really serious about Jesus despite appearing to be. The church, then, becomes individualized. We lose the very center of what once existed, a people defined by our way of life, gathered and marked by a set of practices under allegiance to Jesus Christ.

The last term used by the Nicene Creed to describe the church, *apostolic*, speaks to the "sent-ness" of the church. After the resurrection, in the upper room, right before Jesus breathed the Holy Spirit upon the disciples, he said to them, "As the Father has sent me, so I send you" (John 20:21). In this Jesus described them, the soon-to-be church, as sent ones, extensions of himself, in other words apostles. The Greek word used by Jesus, *apostello*, means "to send." It describes what the church is.

In the ensuing years, the descriptor *apostolic* has been used in two different ways within the church in the West: to describe the missionary practice of the church as a sent people, and to refer to the apostolic succession of authority within the church. In the first meaning, to say that the church is apostolic is to say the church is missionary in its vocation. In other words, the church is always entering its context, recognizing God at work, and extending the gospel into places that have not yet known this God made known in Jesus. *Apostolic* refers to this practice of mission.

In the second meaning, *apostolic* focuses on the continuity of authority and mission to which Jesus commissioned the apostles, which they then handed on to those who followed in leading his mission. The apostle represents the one who sent him or her. The New Testament Scriptures were first recognized as authoritative for the church because they were apostolic documents, written by the apostles, representatives of the one who sent them. The authority to interpret them resided with those in apostolic succession. The process of ordination, after much testing, bestowed authority on a person and deemed him (most of the time it was a "him" by this time) to be within the faithfulness and orthodoxy of apostolic succession.

As the church got more comfortable in **Christendom**, as the culture assumed everybody that wanted to be a Christian already was, the missionary practice of the church receded and the church's focus turned toward its task of apostolic succession. Preservation of the faith took precedence over the extension of the faith.[7] The practice of engaging mission got lost.

To be sure, we must always be concerned with apostolic faithfulness. The church is built on the foundation of the apostles and prophets (Ephesians 2:19-20). But if we lose the actual practice of mission—people discerning God's presence in our neighborhoods; listening to the voices, pains, and sufferings of others in the places where we live; and extending the gospel of Jesus' reign into new places—apostleship will be relegated to issues of right belief only. Apostleship will become something to be enforced. In the process, we will lose the power of the gospel becoming manifest in new and dynamic ways through our way of life in all the places, towns, and villages where we live.

The church began a significant shift at the Council of Nicaea—a shift from a focus on practices to a focus on right belief. The church's *modus operandi* shifted from practicing a way of life together to organizing itself through hierarchical power. The church became less focused on being a local gathering practicing a way of life together and more focused on the large organization enforcing orthodoxy. All this seems to have started as the early church moved from being a group of people marginalized in Roman society to a people culturally accepted by the power of Rome.

## A RETURN TO THE PRACTICES

The Christendom alignment of the church with the state continued beyond the fall of Rome in the fifth century AD. By the end of the medieval period, Christendom dominated Europe. The church was unified and had much power. Then came the Reformation. Leaders like Martin Luther and other reformers charged the Roman Catholic church with corruption and eventually the church became divided between the Roman Catholics, Lutherans, Calvinists, and other dissenters.

The Reformers had to figure out all over again what it meant to be the church. German theologian Philip Melanchthon, with Luther's help, wrote the Augsburg confession. Melanchthon defined the church as existing "wherever the Word of God is properly preached and the sacraments properly administered." Menno Simons, a Dutch Anabaptist reformer, protested this definition, saying that the criterion defining the church should reflect the congregation itself rather than solely the official overseeing it. The church needs to be defined as to how it is different from the world (and the state) rather than simply as an institution alongside others.

Luther adjusted the Augsburg statement in his 1539 publication *On the Councils and Churches* to add several practices, but Menno Simons thought Luther didn't go far enough. Luther, it seemed, couldn't imagine a church that was not sustained and supported by the state. Simons wanted nothing of it. He was working for a church that would be a way of life chosen by disciples of Jesus, a church in mission.[8]

Simons upped the ante and described the church with four practices: 1) *Holy living*—the discernment of concrete moral decisions about how to live, 2) *brotherly love*—which Simons believed happened as a practice around partaking the meal of the Eucharist, 3) *unreserved testimony*—the practice of witnessing to Christ's ways in the world, and 4) *suffering*—the practice of enduring suffering, bearing one another's burdens, and persisting in the face of deprivation as part of discipleship.

The lesson of Menno Simons for us today, and indeed the long history of the church in the West, is that whenever the church no longer sees itself as an institution supported by the state (and other cultural institutions of power), it returns to the shared practices of Christian life for answering the question: What does it mean to be the church? The church is a community of practices that join people together in their submission to Jesus as Lord. To answer the "What is church?" question therefore, we must begin by asking what are those practices?

# 2

# What Is the Church? Further Considerations

All of the above leads us to the question: When beginning a new church, or renewing an existing church, do we start with practices or belief statements?

## PRACTICES OR BELIEF STATEMENTS?

In Christendom, history suggests that Christians assume everybody in the culture is already a Christian (or at least anyone who wants to be). The church defaults to focusing on getting its beliefs right. No longer focused on reaching new peoples for Christ's kingdom, the church turns to keeping existing Christians on the straight and narrow. It's almost irresistible.

But when we are in the context of mission (or post-Christendom), what we are saying no longer makes sense to people who are not Christians. Beliefs, when separated from practices, have over time become rote for Christians.[1] The way they are articulated loses touch with real life because they have not been enfleshed in daily living. This is why, when renewing the church (or planting it over again) in mission, the church must refocus on cultivating the practices of Jesus among a people.

Beliefs cannot make sense to people outside the church without seeing the belief lived in practice.[2] For instance, we can only truly know and share what the atoning work of Christ means for our forgiveness by practicing that forgiveness with someone who has harmed us, or by sharing forgiveness with someone who has been harmed by another. This is how forgiveness will make sense to those outside our faith. We cannot just preach about forgiveness. We must do forgiveness. If the church's beliefs are to make sense again in post-Christendom cultures, the church must return to cultivating the core practices of our Christian life together.

In the philosopher Wittgenstein's terms, the meaning of a word can only be understood in its use. As such, only by living out our beliefs can they make sense to church outsiders. We need to practice forgiving, reconciling, and restoring one another in our marriages, our community, and our conflicts in business and politics, and allow the world to see this great miracle of forgiveness made possible in Jesus' death and resurrection. Only in practicing the forgiveness of Christ will we, and ultimately the world, know what we mean by the belief that in Jesus our sins are forgiven. It is why, if we would return to mission, we must also return to practices.

Another regrettable thing happens when a belief gets extracted from a practice: the belief can become a banner that Christians wave to divide us when we disagree.[3] Not connected to our everyday life any longer, the belief ends up becoming a marker of what certain Christians believe compared to other Christians who do not believe like we do. This is a Christendom phenomenon, as once again Christians become focused on sorting out right belief among fellow Christians instead of focusing on practicing these beliefs in our lives as an offering to the world.

Remember the holiness church mentioned previously that made teetotalism into a belief that defined good Christians in contrast to "those people who drink"? This is an example of Christians taking a good conviction forged out of the practice of discipleship and extracting it into a belief that defines how we are different from other Christians. We can even now use our beliefs to differentiate ourselves from our enemies, and those enemies are often Christians with whom we disagree. If, however, a belief does actual work in our lives, affecting how we live, we can notice the fruit of that belief in people's lives, learn from it, and work out our differences together. In the midst of difference, we can share stories, read Scripture, and discern together how to go forward in the Spirit. The renewal of the church should return us to the practices of Jesus as the foundation by which our faith (and what we believe) can be renewed in Jesus.

We just unpacked what happens when a belief gets extracted from a practice. But what about the dangers of doing the inverse: extracting a practice from a belief? Removing a belief from its practice diminishes the practice and allows it to blend in with the surrounding culture. Pretty soon our prayers to God become prayers to whichever spirit of the age is prevalent. Forgiveness becomes something we do without the cross of Christ and becomes merely a psychotherapeutic technique, devoid of the power and presence of the Holy

Spirit to transform. Making practices central to (re)establishing a church should in no way diminish the importance of right belief, or orthodoxy. They are mutually dependent on each other. Putting practices at the forefront of church formation should not relativize beliefs within a church community. Indeed the beliefs are what make the practices possible.

We see then that beliefs and practices are inextricably intertwined in the life of the church. We must, however, choose which of the two to emphasize when shaping a church. The emphasis shifts when cultural circumstances change. Beliefs tend to take the lead in defining what a church is in the context of Christendom, but in a post-Christendom (or pre-Christendom) context, the church is called into mission, and practices will take the lead in congregational formation. Whether we put the emphasis on belief statements or practices makes all the difference in how we shape a congregation into being what we call the church.[4]

## PROGRAMS OR A WHOLE WAY OF LIFE?

From the practices versus beliefs question comes a second question. Do we organize the church as a set of programs, for individual Christians to access, or as a whole way of life to be lived together in the world?

Here again, history suggests that when the church assumes a Christendom context, it tends to organize the practices as programs in one central place. If the broader culture is assumed to be Christian, a church can focus on helping people be better Christians in their jobs, homes, and volunteer organizations. There is no conflict between these practices and the broader culture, so the church can organize its practices as programs in one central place to fit conveniently into people's present lives.

If on the other hand, the church lives within a non-Christianized culture, the church must organize itself as a whole way of life to be lived in a foreign land, or it surely will not survive. Indeed, if the church wants to engage its neighborhoods, or those who have not yet known Jesus as Lord, or the lostness and brokenness of our culture, its people must live the practices in ways that impact the places where these people's lives intersect. Church leaders therefore must cultivate the practices of Jesus as a whole way of life that can meet the challenges of living in a secular post-Christianized world.

This means that reconciliation, instead of being a centralized program of conflict mediation to equip Christians to lead better lives, will be a practice that shapes our lives in all the places where we live, as a witness to the gospel. We will not only do reconciliation in the confessional booth with the priest before the eucharist or in the mediation office at our local church building. Reconciliation will be a practice that we offer to the world wherever conflict breaks out, wherever sin and evil have contaminated our society. When police have been caught in abuse, this practice will bring police together with the ones abused to reveal sin, lament, repent, forgive, heal, and restore. In the same way, all the practices of Christian living (which we will get to), rather than being the private practices of Christians to be lived on Sunday or in our homes, will shape a way of life that infuses us with the gospel. It is important then, in answering the "What is church?" question, to consider carefully: Will we organize the church around a set of programs offered in a central place or as a whole way of life to be lived together in the world?

## COERCION OR PRESENCE?

History shows that whenever the church lives comfortably in a Christendom world it tends to organize itself as a hierarchy. However, when the church is not aligned with the worldly powers, and is living as a minority people, it tends to organize itself in mutuality. A third question thus emerges, how shall we view and organize authority within the church?

After Constantine, a coercive form of leadership took root in the church. Rather than conflicts over beliefs being worked out in communities of practices with mutual conversation, the church moved toward requiring its members to assent to specific beliefs. There is a certain power over people in this approach. Whenever a belief is challenged, even today we find ourselves answering with the words "We believe this because. . ." rather than "We do this because we believe. . ." If people have questions, or worse, dare to challenge the church's beliefs, they are accused of heresy by leaders in the church and possibly even removed from the church. The church has become focused on enforcing orthodoxy instead of working it out mutually among a people. This approach works well in holding the church together in Christendom, but it does not work in the same way when Christendom culture no longer exists.

Today, as the culture has shifted, and the Christian's beliefs are challenged, churches are tempted to enforce orthodoxy as if it still held Christendom-like power. Defensiveness rears its ugly head. In some so-called fundamentalist churches, members are pressured to assent to the church's beliefs and to the specific way they are articulated or be damned to the fires of hell. Talk about coercion! Often resentment, push-back, or even a complete revulsion toward faith happens among the young in these kinds of churches. When beliefs are separated from practices, coercion sneaks in and beliefs lose their currency. In the process, why those beliefs were important gets lost.

And so, it is more important than ever for churches to work out their life together mutually in the very presence of Jesus. This does not mean that there is no authority in the church. Rather, the authority is of the Spirit and works through conviction as opposed to coercion. The gifts of the Spirit are set loose to lead. The teachers teach, the preachers preach, the prophets prophecy, the pastors pastor, and on we go with each member contributing according to the measure of grace given to each person (Romans 12:6-8). This is shared leadership carried out in mutuality. We submit ourselves one to another out of reverence for the Lordship of Christ at work among us (Ephesians 4:21). Together we have the mind of Christ (1 Corinthians 2:16). The Spirit works. And then someone says, like the apostles once did in Acts 15, "It seemed good to the Holy Spirit and to us." We do not enforce beliefs on people; we work out our beliefs together.

When a belief is challenged, there is no need for the church's leaders to clamp down on questioners as if they should exercise authority over someone. We eat together, are present to one another, allow all the gifted ones around the table to present the issues and contribute their wisdom. We hear all voices, and we dialogue in and through the mutuality of the gifts. These are the foundational practices for being the church in these times. In this process our beliefs are enriched and deepened in a community by the Spirit. We become less defensive, more inclusive.

In Christendom, the church could get by functioning under the authority of a hierarchy. Those sitting in church services had been trained for many years to respect the authority of the one in charge. This approach to church leadership was efficient. As with the monarchy of Israel (which God allowed as a concession in 1 Samuel 8), God can work with and around hierarchies.

But ultimately, hierarchy is not God's way. Ultimately the church is defined by another way. It runs by another power: the power of the presence of God revealed in and through Christ at work in a people. And so Jesus instructs the disciples, after they ask him one more time for worldly power (Mark 10:37), "You know that those who are supposed to rule over the Gentiles lord it over them, and their great men exercise authority over them. But it shall not be so among you; but whoever would be great among you must be your servant" (Mark 10:42-43 RSV). Likewise, in a similar situation, where the disciples asked him for worldly power, Jesus (Luke 22:29-30) points them to the practice of the table—where they could learn about mutuality and authority and where he washed their feet. Jesus was teaching them that it is in these practices that we learn to mutually submit one to another, and to him so that he can work his kingdom among us. It is in these spaces that a church can be renewed once the hierarchy, still remaining from the era of Christendom, passes away.

## WHAT ARE THESE PRACTICES?

One last question must be considered in leading a church to renew the "what" of a practicing community of Jesus: What exactly are these practices?

Beginning in the New Testament, and proceeding down through the church's history, we can identify practices present wherever there is a church. Elsewhere I have argued for the following seven practices as distinctive of the church (each listed with a founding text):

1. The Lord's table (Luke 22:14-30; 24:13-35)
2. Reconciliation (Matthew 18:15-20)
3. Proclaiming the gospel (Luke 10:1-16)
4. Being with the least of these (Matthew 25:31-46)
5. The fivefold gifting (Ephesians 4:1-16)
6. Being with children (Matthew 18:1-5)
7. Kingdom prayer (Matthew 6:9-13) [5]

Each practice embodies (and depends on) major doctrines of the Christian faith. The Lord's table teaches us about the atonement, forgiveness, incarnation, and new life in Christ. Proclaiming the gospel teaches us how Jesus became Lord, who he is, what he has done, and how he now reigns and is at work among us. Reconciliation teaches us about forgiveness, God's love, and the atonement in Christ. All the major doctrines of the Nicene Creed are taught and learned through these practices of the church. Belief is inextricably intertwined with practices.

A Catholic reader might recognize overlap between these seven practices and what eventually became the seven sacraments of the Western Roman Catholic church. They are similar except that these seven practices do not include baptism and marriage, two sacraments that are initiatory, not meant to be repeated, at least not in a weekly fashion. The seven practices listed above are all regular, ongoing, repetitive practices in everyday life. And yet, even if we combined these practices with the sacraments, we still would not have an exhaustive list of the church's practices down through history. One church historian has noted that in the twelfth century some churches in Europe listed as many as thirty practices as regular sacraments of the church.[6] Nonetheless, I believe these seven core practices alongside the initiatory rites cover the basics for

shaping a way of life that is profoundly lived in the presence
and reign of Christ.

I have argued elsewhere that these practices encompass a
whole way of life.[7] Eating (the Lord's table), conflict (reconciliation), the need for hope and seeing God at work (proclaiming the gospel), sustenance through economic and bodily
hardship (being with the least of these), leadership (the gifts),
raising children (being with children), and walking with God
in all things (kingdom prayer) are all parts of life we experience regularly. These are practices that we do on Sunday but
also as part of everyday life, so they shape the way we live the
rest of the week as well. We will cover how this takes place as
church in chapter 3.

The work of each church then, is to discern which practices
will guide each church's life. Each practice must be grounded
from Scripture in the words and life of Jesus. Each practice
must have a history in the life of the church. Each practice
must make way for the presence of Christ to be made manifest
by the Spirit. These practices are the foundation for what it
means to be a church.

# 3

# Why Church? Presence Is How God Works

Why participate in church? Why go to all the trouble? Do Christians actually need the church? Couldn't we just each do our own personal Bible studies and be done with church? And when it comes to justice, isn't that the government's job? Why do we need the church anyway? While we're at it, why does God need the church? You would think God could accomplish everything and anything he wanted to without a church. God could put a chip in people's brains and communicate directly to people. Tell them to get busy or else. Was it not the Protestants who argued for a long time that there is no mediator between God and humans except Jesus Christ? Why then do we even need church?

Many are asking these kinds of questions today, subtly or not so subtly. Faced with the many failures of the church in the West, surely we and God can do better without it?

And so every church, every group of Christians seeking to renew the church, must answer the "Why?" question. It is unavoidable because the "What is church?" question (the first two chapters) only becomes important if we have a compelling answer to why we should participate in church in the first place.

## THE WAY GOD WORKS

The fundamental answer to the "Why church" question is: Presence is the way God works. Therefore, for God to work the way he chooses to work, requires a people for God to be present to, and to make space for God to be made known in the world. God's presence works in and through social relationships, therefore God needs a social network to be present to and through, because it is by God's presence that he chooses to work in the world. God's chosen social network is the church. The whole of Scripture testifies to the reality that presence is the way God works.

From the beginning, God created the garden of Eden as "a place where God dwells and man [sic] should worship him."[1] Humanity was created to be in God's presence and Eden was God's sanctuary.[2] Presence was the way God existed among humanity. But Adam and Eve usurped God and soon violence broke out (Genesis 6:5). God's presence was broken, and God withdrew that presence. The violence of the Noahic flood resulted.

But soon thereafter, God set out to restore his presence again with creation. God's first act was to call Abraham and birth a people named (eventually) Israel to bless the nations. God would be present to this people, restore this people, show the world what true restoration looks like through this people.

Many ups and downs ensued along the way.[3] Years later, after being enslaved under a foreign power, God freed the people and Moses led them out of Egypt. They found themselves at Mount Sinai where they lost faith in God and made a golden calf and worshiped it. Up in the clouds of Mount Sinai God angrily told Moses to lead Israel on without his presence because they had blasphemed God's name. Moses responded to God by saying, "If Your presence does not go with us, do not lead us up from here. . . Is it not by Your going with us. . . that we, I and Your people, may be distinguished from all the other people who are on the face of the earth?" (Exodus 33:15-16 NASB). It could not be any more plain. God's people are not his people apart from his presence. It is through God's presence that God works among them and through them.

And so God relented and went *with* his people. They built a traveling tabernacle to house God's presence among the people. God's presence guided them, encouraged them, and led them through the wilderness. Years later, in the promised land, the temple stood in the center of Jerusalem as the meeting place of the nation with God's presence. This is where the people came to be reconciled with God, to be present with God, to pray in the presence of God. God's presence is at the core of the way God works among his people. God chooses a people Israel, just as he chooses a people the church, as part of the way God works through his presence.

When God's people rebelled and forsook him all over again for false idols, God withdrew his presence again (Ezekiel 10). The people were dispersed into exile and the temple of God's presence was destroyed. Nonetheless, God promised to renew his presence among his people someday (Ezekiel 37:27). This is the nature of how God works: God's love is great, God's compassion never fails, God's mercies are new every morning

(Lamentations 3:22-23). God is not violent, never coerces, is ever patient, ever pursuing, and never gives up. Over and over again, through the major and minor prophets, God promises to renew his presence once the time of suffering and consequences is over. Presence is the way God chooses to work, and God is ever calling a people to return to himself, promising to make his presence known.4

God delivered on that promise in sending the Son to take on flesh. In the opening gospel, Jesus is born of the virgin Mary and, as foretold by the prophet, "they shall name him Immanuel," which means "God with us" (Matthew 1:23 NASB). God has come in flesh to be the very presence of God among us. The gospel of John describes this same dynamic, announcing "the Word became flesh, and dwelt [tabernacled] among us" (John 1:14 NASB). In the language of the tabernacle in the wilderness, the gospel writer declares that the living God has come to dwell among God's people again. This is the way God will save the world. This is the way God works.

Jesus lives, dies, and rises from the dead conquering death, sin, and evil. And he ascends to rule the world through his presence. In the farewell discourses of John's gospel, Jesus tells the disciples that though he goes, he will not "leave [them] as orphans" (John 14:18 NASV). Instead the Holy Spirit will come in his place (John 16:5ff) and by the Spirit he shall be with them. The Father and the Son by the Spirit will make their "abode" with them (John 14:23). "Abide in me as I abide in you," Jesus tells them (John 15:4). God's presence has been renewed to them and to us in Jesus Christ by the Spirit. God is shaping a people, the church, to be present to and through.

In the upper room, as the resurrected Jesus communes with the disciples, he says, "As the Father has sent me, so I send you." And then he breathes on them the Holy Spirit (John 20:21-22).

God's very presence, in and through Jesus, extends into the world through these disciples, the foundation of what is to become the church. The church shall be the extension of the promise made to Israel to renew God's presence among them.

At the feast of Pentecost, God pours out the Spirit's presence on a large gathering, men and women, sons and daughters, prophets and prophetesses (Acts 2). The church is born. God has come to be present among God's people. According to the apostle Paul, we are the church, God's own people, a "temple" in the midst of the world (2 Corinthians 6:16). We are no longer strangers to God, but citizens of "the household of God," being knit together into "a holy temple in the Lord . . . for a dwelling place of God in the Spirit" (Ephesians 2:21-22 RSV). God's presence in Jesus does not end with Jesus' resurrection and ascension. God's presence extends in Jesus to a people, his church, as they are sent into the world (John 20:21-23). Jesus says, "Go, therefore, into the whole world. . . ," charging listeners to complete the mission until the end of the age (Matthew 28).

In the final chapter of Revelation, we see where this is all heading: the new heaven and the new earth, a place where God dwells *among* the people so that there will be no need for a temple. Indeed, the new heaven and earth are described in terms of the dimensions of the temple, the dwelling place of God among Israel.[5] And so the voice says in Revelation 21:3, "See, the home of God is among mortals. He will dwell with them; they will be his peoples, and God himself will be with them" (NRSV). This is the goal of God's redemptive work. This is the mission: God's presence floods the joining of the new heaven with the new earth and all will be made new. From beginning to end, the whole of Scripture testifies that it is by God's presence that God works in and through a people and restores the world.

The Psalms speak to this theme repeatedly. One of my favorites is Psalm 46:

> God is our refuge and strength, a very *present* help in trouble . . . There is a river whose streams make glad the city of God, The holy *dwelling* places of the Most High. God *is in the midst of her*, she will not be moved; God will help her when morning dawns. The nations made an uproar, the kingdoms tottered; He raised His voice, the earth melted. The Lord of hosts is *with* us . . . He makes wars to cease to the end of the earth; He breaks the bow and cuts the spear in two; He burns the chariots with fire. "Cease striving and know that I am God. I will be exalted among the nations, I will be exalted in the earth." The Lord of hosts is *with* us; The God of Jacob is our stronghold. (NASB, italics added)

Notice the words "with," "in the midst," "present," and "dwelling" in this text. These words are used throughout the Bible to show God's real presence to dispel violence, to bring peace, and to cease striving. God works in and through his presence, bringing the richness of love, reconciliation, and justice, and never forcing himself on the people. It is by God's presence that God shall change the world. And it is for this work that God's presence requires a people. The church, as the extension from Israel, is this people.

The recognition that God chooses to work through his presence—that God's power is made manifest in his presence, that indeed God accomplishes powerful transformation in the lives of people and the systems they live in all through his presence—singularly answers the question "Why do we need the church?" Presence works through social relationships between people and God, people and people, and people and systems. God disrupts, heals, and renews people and systems not through coercion over people but by his very presence among and with people. And for God to work this way, God requires a people to be present to and to make space for his presence in the world. God requires the church.[6]

## WHAT IS PRESENCE?

When asked "What is 'presence'?" I often refer to a simple mundane practice of having breakfast with my son Max every Saturday morning. We've been doing this since he started eating real food. Max and I both have our problems keeping our attention on any one thing. Through the years, I have often struggled to gain my son's attention as I sit across from him at the breakfast table. I'd be sure to choose a booth in the restaurant where he could not be distracted by the television mounted on the wall. I'd insist on no phones at the table (if we had them). Nonetheless, given that we're both plagued by attention deficits of various kinds, nothing I'd do could quite capture his attention. He'd be ever looking someplace else other than me.

Then I started to develop a practice of praying as we sat there at the table. I'm not referring to a prayer of thanksgiving over the food, which is itself a worthy practice. My prayer was more akin to the prayer of epiclesis that a priest prays in presiding over the eucharist. In this prayer, a priest invokes the presence of Christ at the table and prays for Christ to make his presence real. And so I'd pray a version of that prayer quietly, often just to myself, saying, "Lord, be present here at this table" or "Lord, help me tend to your presence here as we eat," or "Lord, help me be present to your presence in Max."

As I prayed, I would sense my attention move onto Max. A calm would come over my body and I would feel the sense of Jesus' very presence inhabiting our space together. I found myself freed from distractions and able to give myself fully to Max and to Jesus at work here in this space. I was able to just be there, patiently, waiting for Max to be there too with me. Often Max would sense this unusual presence. Often within seconds, he'd notice my presence with him. His eyes would quit moving and become present to me too. God was doing something here at this table. In this moment, a moment of supernatural connection, God could work between us in amazing ways by the power of the Holy Spirit in this space.

As mundane as that breakfast table is, I believe it models how God's presence wants to invade and work among the many social spaces we live in every day of our lives. It is via this same presence that God can move, shake up, speak, use people, and shape meetings at the local village zoning committee, the union hall, the protest marches in the midst of racial violence, the shelter for homeless folk where we are sharing meals and stories of the way God works. It could be domestic violence, it could be built-up racist animus between a neighborhood and its police. Whatever the social spaces we enter, as we make space for God's presence, God can disrupt, open ears, and work among all the violence, antagonism, pain, and brokenness for reconciliation, healing, and renewal.

This is the way God wants to work in our lives, our neighborhoods, our cities. But God requires that people make space for him, sense him, discern him, recognize him as God is working, and invite others into this new thing God is doing. The question is who will be present to God's presence at work? Who will engage in practices of God's presence like eating breakfast with the hurting and the poor, sharing space for economic and social reconciliation, praying for healing of broken relationships and strife, and so much more?

The church can uniquely know God's presence and make space for God at work in the world. The church is uniquely gifted with practices that make space for Jesus to be present and work for healing, transformation, and renewal of all things. God's presence is the answer to the why question. It is why the church is indispensable to God's mission to renew the world.

# 4

# Why Church?
# God's Mission

God's mission is to restore all creation to God's presence. As the writer of Revelation foresees, a new heaven and new earth is coming (Revelation 21:1), and this city will not have a temple (Revelation 21:22), for God will live fully with humanity (Revelation 21:3). This is where God is taking the world.

But isn't God's mission about bringing the kingdom of God to completion over the whole earth? Isn't building the kingdom of God the mission Christians are called to in the world? What does God's kingdom have to do with presence? Why does God's kingdom require the church? How the church fits into this kingdom mission answers much about the "Why church?" question.

## THE KINGDOM AND GOD'S PRESENCE

Much has been written about the Jewish expectations for God's kingdom at the time of Jesus.[1] As the prophets foretold, the day would come eventually when "the Lord will become king over all the earth" (Zechariah 14:9). God's judgment would come, God's rule would be restored, and peace, justice, healing, and renewal would follow. Jesus came preaching that this kingdom had begun (Mark 1:14-15). It was his dominant message. This was God's mission.

Today, two thousand years later, the image of "the kingdom of God" might imply to some that God is going to change the world through overwhelming force, not the way of presence we have been describing above. A king's rule is hierarchical after all. Typically, kings enforce their will on people in some way. Is this God's preferred way in the kingdom?

But, as seen in the Bible, God's noncoercive presence precedes chronologically any idea of a kingdom rule "over." This chronology gives us key insights into how God is carrying out the mission of his kingdom. Remember that the tabernacle, the symbol of God's presence among Israel, precedes the monarchy of Israel. God had ruled among the people for many years by his presence through prophets, priests, and judges. But Israel became impatient with how inefficient this all seemed. They demanded a king like the rest of the nations to rule over them, get things done faster, and accomplish justice. At least this is what they thought.

Samuel resisted giving Israel a king like this. But God told him to do it anyway, saying, "they have not rejected you (Samuel). . . they have rejected me from being king over them" (1 Samuel 8:7). Giving Israel a king was a concession by God to Israel.[2] This kingship could never replace the presence of God, and Israel would later regret having a king (1 Samuel

8:9). Years later, after the debacle of the monarchies, Israel returned from exile and the temple was rebuilt but the monarchy was not restored. God's calling for the rebuilding of the temple, but not the restoring of the monarchy, is a call for Israel to return to his presence.

With the coming of Jesus, God did not discard the kingdom idea but rather changed it from Israel's prior ways. God, in sending the Son, fulfilled the idea of God's rule as his presence among us. Jesus comes to be king but will rule like no other king. He will work powerfully through his presence. This should not be interpreted as Jesus ruling through the personal piety of his followers only. Jesus' power will move mountains (Mark 11:23). His presence will break down the strongholds of evil and heal the nations. He will do all of this by his presence.

As he inaugurates the table, Jesus tells the disciples, "As my father has conferred on me, so I confer on you a kingdom" (Luke 22:29, my translation). Jesus is initiating the disciples into a new way of kingdom, a new way of getting things done. He is turning the whole idea of kingdom and how it works upside down.[3] "The kings of the Gentiles lord it over them . . . But not so with you," Jesus says (Luke 22:25-26, NRSV). Instead, this table, in his presence, foreshadows the reign of God. It is in and through his presence among the disciples, in a social space like the table, that this kingdom shall come to be. Jesus is teaching the disciples that whenever they make space for his presence in their midst, his power will be made manifest and his kingdom will take shape.

## IT TAKES A CHURCH

The church, this people who makes space for his presence, is at the very center of God bringing this unique kingdom into the world. It is the foretaste of the kingdom, a witness to the kingdom, and the bringer of the kingdom into the world.

At the turn of the last century, famous theologian and pastor Walter Rauschenbusch argued that the message of the kingdom of God had gotten lost for Christians and the church itself had replaced it.[4] Rauschenbusch worried that the church had become the goal of Christianity, not the bringing of the kingdom of God to earth in Jesus' name. But it is a mistake to separate the church from Christ's kingdom completely like Rauschenbusch does. It is not like the church can work something (the kingdom) in the world that the church itself is not already being.

A people gathered around a table, a people submitted to God's reign, a people who make space for God's presence and kingship: this is the church. In church, people's lives are changed, broken relationships are reconciled, people's bodies are healed, racism is exposed and confessed and vanquished, the poor among us are fed and begin to flourish, God's reign becomes visible for the neighborhood to see, and God's rule spreads like wildfire through the towns and the villages and even the higher echelons of power and wealth. All of this happens in the power of God's presence. The church is the people God uses to make space for Jesus' presence and for God's rule to be made visible wherever we are present in the world.[5] It is the answer to the question "Why church?"

Surely God can choose to order the affairs of humanity in other ways. Just as God used Cyrus to move the people of Israel back to Jerusalem and rebuild the temple, God can work through worldly power to achieve his purposes (Isaiah 45). Nonetheless, God ultimately works redemptively through his own nonviolent presence. And so the church is central to God's mission in the world.

It is at this point that we might be tempted to say that the church is on a mission from God, but this would be an overstep. Once we realize that it is by God's presence at work in the world that God's power and mission are accomplished, we realize that church can never take God's mission into its own hands. All we can do is open space for God's presence to work and be recognized, and then for us to join in with God. Any attempt to take God's mission into our own hands usurps God and undercuts his power.

The church, therefore, is not on a mission from God; it is God that is on a mission and the church is invited to participate. As German theologian Jurgen Moltmann once put it: the church does not have a mission, "it is the mission of the Son and the Spirit through the Father that includes the church."[6] God himself, the **triune God**, has extended himself via the Son and the Spirit into the world to save and restore the world, and invited the church into his very life for the sake of mission. God invites us into his movement, his mission to make himself know by his presence and to restore the whole world. It is the "why" of the church. It is utterly, unspeakably marvelous.

## GOD'S MISSION AS FULLNESS

In his letter to the Ephesians, the apostle Paul describes the church (Christ's "body") as "the fullness of him who fills all in all" (Ephesians 1:23). With these words Paul places the church at the very center of Christ's presence in the whole world. The church and the world are both places filled by Christ's presence, but there's something special going on in the church that Paul calls the "fullness."[7]

"Fullness" (the word *pleroma* in Greek) alludes to the Shekinah glory of God's presence in the holy of holies in the temple of Israel.[8] Just as God's presence is full in the temple, so

Christ manifests his special presence viscerally, intensely, and visibly among the church. Yet Christ's presence is not confined to the location of the church (just as God's presence is not confined to the temple for Israel[9]). His presence is at work in the whole world, yet the people of God, subject to Jesus as Lord, open space for his presence to become visible among them wherever they go. Jesus is present over the whole world (his **omnipresence**) but he becomes visibly present (**manifest presence**) wherever his people meet to make space for him to work.

This picture of the church in Ephesians gets to the heart of the "Why church?" question. The church is the instrument God uses to make space for Jesus' presence to become visible in the world. As Ephesians 1:22 says, God has made Jesus "head over all things for the church." Jesus is indeed Lord over the whole world, but it is through the church, through its submission to Christ's lordship, that his omnipresence over the whole world can be made manifest and work for healing and transformation. The church is the essential relational space for God to work in the way he has chosen to change the world.

## THE TWOFOLD MOVEMENT OF THE SON

This omnipresence/manifest presence dynamic is a work of the triune God. The Father sends the Son into the world. Jesus Christ the Son lives, dies, and is resurrected. The powers of sin, death, and evil are defeated. And then a twofold movement begins. First, Jesus ascends to the right hand of the Father to rule "until he has put all enemies under his feet" (1 Corinthians 15:25). He rules as the lamb that was slain (Revelation 5:12-13), not a despot monarch, but by his omnipresence over the whole world until the mission is complete. But also, a second movement begins. Jesus sends out the church (John 20:21-22) into every nook and cranny of the world as the means by which his presence shall be made manifest in a visible way.[10] He extends his presence by the Spirit (who takes Jesus' place, John 16:5ff). The church, as subjects of the king, makes relational social space for his presence to become manifest. In so doing, the church is caught up into the mission of the triune God. Kingdom breaks in. Miracles happen. The world sees and joins in. God's omnipresent rule over the whole world is made manifest locally wherever the church is faithful to God's presence.[11]

The great commission (Matthew 28:16-20) testifies to this twofold movement of Jesus' omnipresence and manifest presence. Before he ascends, Jesus announces, "All authority in heaven and on earth has been given to me" (v.18). There couldn't be a more sweeping statement of his omnipresent rule over the whole earth. Under these auspices, Jesus sends his disciples out ("Go therefore") into his mission. He is at work over the whole world, drawing people to himself by his presence. But Jesus also says, "Remember, I am *with* you always, even to the completion [my translation] of the age" (v. 20). Jesus will be specially present with the disciples as they go. By his manifest presence, Jesus' disciples will be empowered, releasing Jesus' work of reconciling, restoring, and healing the world until the mission is complete.

This is the "why" of the church's existence! God is present over the whole world but chooses to make this presence visible through a people called "church." Here, amid the social spaces of God's people in the world, submitting to Jesus as Lord, God becomes viscerally present and is able to do amazing things he could do nowhere else.

## BEING FAITHFUL TO HIS PRESENCE

The Western world today has largely architected God out of our existence. The average person has little awareness that God's presence is near, waiting to push into our awareness. We live daily as if God does not exist.

We work long hours at our jobs. We manage our family's affairs, shuttling children to and from various sports programs, tutoring sessions, and school functions. Our paychecks enter our bank accounts. We pay our bills. We solve problems. And when we can, we go to a church service, trying to fit God into our busy lives, with the hope that God can somehow help us get through another week successfully. Jesus is like a little sprinkle we put on top of the cake of our already predetermined busy lives. We have little awareness that God in Jesus Christ longs to break in and transform our world. Instead we are locked into our lives of convenience, comfort, and security while the world lumbers on in its brokenness, injustice, darkness, loneliness, and pain. We are oblivious to God. In the words of Isaiah, God is saying to us: "I was ready to be sought out by those who did not ask, to be found by those who did not seek me. I said, 'Here I am, here I am,' to a nation that did not call on my name" (Isaiah 65:1-2).

Yet the church is called to be the church again: "the fullness of him who fills all in all." We must open space amid our lives to God's presence. We must be God's faithful presence. As I have said elsewhere, "faithful presence names the reality that God is present in the world and that he uses a people faithful to his presence to make himself concrete and real amid the world's struggles and pain."[12] The church is the practice of faithful presence and it is the definitive answer to the "Why church?" question.

The question that remains is "How?" To this we now turn.

# 5

# How Do We Do Church? Social Spaces

If the "what" and the "why" questions have been answered, the "how" question now moves front and center. *How* do we organize a church to fulfill the mission we have been invited into? The answer should be quite simple: go and cultivate these practices among a people. But there is so much more to say beyond this.

## WE NEED SOCIAL SPACES

The practices, mentioned in chapter 2, are not only (or merely) practices of personal discipleship. They are inherently social. They require a social gathering of some sort to do them. Surely these practices require the discipling of individuals into these practices. But it is more than this, because each practice opens space for Christ to manifest his presence among a group of people. And so, as organizers of the church, we need social spaces, groups of people who gather to do the practices together in all of life.

The seven practices, mentioned in chapter 2, all bring people together into a social space to submit to Jesus as Lord. The Lord's table, reconciliation, proclaiming gospel, being with the least of these, the gifts of leadership, being with children, and kingdom prayer all create a social space between people where Jesus' presence can work. Although each practice shapes us personally—in how we eat, read the Bible, pray, etc.—as individuals, this formation only starts as we gather in groups. In these practices, Jesus' presence can shape and use the interactions between people. It is not just "I" who encounter Jesus in the practice, it is "we" as Christians who encounter the living Christ in the social spaces created by these practices.

In Matthew 18:15-20, the practice of reconciliation brings at least "two or three" people together. They gather "in his name," to submit to his authority as Lord and king. A social reality is formed amid the conflict. The person who has been sinned against goes directly to the sinner, face to face ("when the two of you are alone") and a social space occurs. If agreement does not happen, another friend is invited to listen (v. 16). If still no agreement, then another. A group forms not against someone but through mutual listening and discerning. When listening and agreement happen, Jesus declares, "I am there among" you. He becomes manifestly present in this social space. And what is bound on earth shall be bound in heaven, what is loosed on earth shall be loosed in heaven (Matthew 18:15-20). The very power of Jesus' reign is released into this social space to change the world. Human relations are disrupted and rearranged. The forgiveness and reconciliation made possible in Jesus Christ become real. A future is opened up.

This is the way all the practices work. The social spaces of our lives take shape by these practices. The Lord's table requires that we reconcile with anyone we have enmity toward before we come to eat (Matthew 5:24; 1 Corinthians 11: 29-30). We are told to eat with someone at a table before we proclaim the gospel (Luke 10:8, 9). The practice of being with the poor socially opens space for Jesus to say, "I am there with you" (my paraphrase, Matthew 25:40). The gifts of the Spirit's authority are shared as members one to another in a social body (Ephesians 4:7-12). Indeed, all the practices open social spaces for Christ to come and be manifestly present and work among us. Any answer to the "How do we do church?" question must address facilitating social spaces for the practices so that Christ can become present and work in manifest ways.

## HIS PRESENCE AMIDST THE PLACES OF OUR LIVES

Historically, the church has always believed that Jesus comes to be present among his people when they gather, specifically when Christians do the core practices together like reconciliation. During the Middle Ages the European church referred to the presence of Jesus in the social spaces of these practices as his "real presence." Roman Catholics believed that Jesus' "real presence" materializes at the table (they eventually called this transubstantiation). The bread and wine actually become the body and blood of Jesus.[1] And so the practice of the table, along with the other practices of the Roman Catholic Church, were eventually called sacraments, meaning they are material realities (outward signs), given (instituted) by Christ to minister the presence of Christ (to give grace) into the various circumstances and situations of our lives. The Reformed

churches also had a version of this same belief regarding the
Lord's table.

As the Christian faith moved into modern contexts, Pentecostal and holiness movements (among others) emphasized
the inward experience of Christ's presence. John Wesley (and
his brother Charles) famously had an experience of being
"strangely warmed" inwardly by the Spirit at a group meeting at Aldersgate, London. When this movement traveled to
North America, many holiness groups recognized that there is
a second work of grace, a filling of the Spirit, an inward experience of the presence of Jesus that comes to every believer
after salvation. Since then, this presence of Jesus by the Spirit
has become known among many kinds of holiness, Pentecostal, and evangelical Christians, as a personal inward experience. Some churches today even focus on the special presence
of Christ as the inward experience that happens as we sing
together in a worship service.

In distinction from Roman Catholics and Holiness Pentecostals, Anabaptists have emphasized communal social spaces
as the place of his presence. Anabaptists rejected the Roman
Catholic view of transubstantiation because they feared the
church (and the priest) could control Christ's presence and
use this control for worldly purposes. Some Anabaptists likewise feared that the inward experience was too emotional and
open to manipulation. In modern times, some Anabaptists
notice that the Roman Catholic sacramental and the evangelical inward memorial experience around the Lord's table
individualize the presence of Christ, as the bread and the cup
can be offered to Christians individually or the inward experience can be too focused on oneself.

Distinctively, many Anabaptists have focused on the pot-
luck meal as the center of church life. In an intensely social

experience, Anabaptists see that Christ's presence comes to be with his people when they eat in Christian fellowship. This Anabaptist focus, on the social space of eating as the site of his presence, easily transfers to all the key practices of the church. In all the practices, a social space is opened for Christ's presence to be made real. Anabaptist theologian John Howard Yoder therefore described these practices of the church as "**social sacraments**."[2] According to Yoder, Christ becomes specially present "in and with, through and under what men and women do" together in these practices.[3]

"Social sacraments" overcome many of the problems inherent in the other two understandings of Christ's presence in the church (Roman Catholic and Pentecostal). In mutual community, the presence of Jesus cannot be controlled by the priest (as some have accused the Roman Catholics of doing). This presence only comes to us as the community submits together to Jesus. Likewise, in mutual community the presence of Christ cannot be manipulated as an easily internalized emotion (as Catholics and Anglo-Catholics have accused the Pentecostals of doing). Any emotion must become the product of a social gathering that chastens and shapes one's experience before the living Christ. And yet the truth in these two other traditions—that Jesus' presence is real and experienced—is incorporated and the excesses corrected through the recognition that it takes a group of people mutually submitted to Christ and one another to know him and his presence, and be sustained, empowered, and transformed therein. The shaping of these social spaces is integral to the "how" of organizing the church.

## CHRISTENDOM VERSUS POST-CHRISTENDOM ORGANIZATION

But if the "how" question is answered by "We must cultivate social spaces," the question remains, "Where?" Do we organize these social spaces in one location or do we disperse the social spaces across neighborhoods and among the lost and hurting?

As already mentioned, most churches' first instinct is to organize these practices at one central location. By gathering everyone at one central place, churches anticipate that this makes for better teaching (the best ordained teachers can teach everybody) and more efficient teaching (getting more people trained at one time). Often churches organize these practices as programs that Christians can access at one central place at their convenience, kind of like a grocery store accumulates foods, goods, and services in one central place. In the process, we focus on training individual Christians who come to our central location to access the training. We ignore the important task of cultivating the social spaces in our lives where the risen Jesus can become present and work.

It is not necessarily bad to train individuals or to make this training convenient for Christians to access. Practical considerations have their place. But centralizing the training of the practices and making it convenient to individuals is a decidedly Christendom habit of organizing. It assumes that there are many Christians who will want to come to a large central gathering place for a training session. It assumes that these same Christians can go back into the world and survive as individuals in living out these practices. Putting all the emphasis on a central location subtly implies that our social life outside church is nice but not absolutely necessary. In a Christianized culture, we can afford to train people to flourish as Christians individually in a culture that is friendly to them. They do not require the support that social spaces can provide.

In post-Christendom, however, we can no longer assume that people, especially if they are new to Christianity, are willing to drive to and gather in a central place called the church to participate in a program. In addition, the world today is a challenging place for Christians, trained or otherwise, to survive on their own as individuals. We need social spaces where people can grow, flourish, and give witness to the kingdom of God in their neighborhoods, workplaces, schools, and the places of the hurting and disenfranchised. In post-Christendom, we are ever aware of the injustices, struggles, pain, and brokenness around us. The church needs to organize social spaces where the justice and mercy of the kingdom of Christ can become manifest there as well. The church needs to cultivate social spaces so that Christians can live a whole way of life that witnesses to the transforming good news of Jesus Christ to our neighbors.

This demands a different answer to the "how" question than has been common in Christendom's history. It is to this we now turn.

# 6

# How Do We Do Church? Three Places

The New Testament church described its organization this way: "Day by day, as they spent much time together in the temple, they broke bread at home and ate their food with glad and generous hearts, praising God and having the goodwill of all the people. And day by day the Lord added to their number those who were being saved" (Acts 2:46-47).

Notice that the church is not gathering in a central location only. They lived their lives together "day by day." For these early believers, church is not a Sunday morning gathering at a central place, it is a whole way of life. Although they did spend much time in the temple, a centralized place for all Israel, they also gathered in homes (or as some versions say "from house to house") and they were known by people outside their faith ("all the people") with a fondness ("having the goodwill") which suggests a familiarity that comes from regular presence

with these people. It seems therefore that this church organized its life in three places: the temple, the home, and among
all the people.[1]

The text explains that the church "devoted themselves" to
practices in these various places, which included studying the
apostles' teaching, fellowshipping, breaking bread, and praying (v. 42). They "broke bread," as some versions say, from
"house to house" (v. 46), and so they practiced their life in
and among the neighborhoods. They lived their lives "day by
day" and, by being among those outside the church, "the Lord
added to their number those who were being saved" (v. 47).
This is the essence of "how do we do church" in mission.

## NOT PROGRAMS BUT (THREE) PLACES

If we would organize the church for mission, then, we must
organize the church not as a program to attend in one centralized place but in three places. The church is not a set of
programs for individuals but is a whole way of life cultivated
in three places. Elsewhere I have described these three places
as three circles where the church cultivates her life in the
practices.[2]

*The close circle.* Represented by "the temple" in Acts 2:46,
this is the circle of committed Christians who gather to submit their lives to his lordship in worship and community. It
is described as "close," not because the circle is closed, but
because it offers the closest of fellowship. This close fellowship is made possible because all who gather here are committed (as those who go to the temple) to discern their relationship to Jesus as Lord and to one another in a reconciled
close communion.

In Luke 22, Jesus hosts the close table. He points to the
table and tells the disciples of the new kind of kingdom taking

place here (vv. 28-30). It is the sweetest of communions, yet there is also disruption, truth-telling, and conflict (vv. 22-24, 31-34). This is the kind of close authentic fellowship where God works. Jesus is at the center of this place. He is the host. As they practice the table together, there is a supernatural closeness with his presence.

In this close circle we gather not only around the eating at the table but around the other practices, including the preaching of the Word, mutual reconciliation and sharing, the gifts of the Spirit, and the being with children. We submit to Jesus and he comes to be present and work among us. This is the place of worship. We learn to recognize his presence here via the practices. It is ground zero for the kingdom.

*The dotted circle.* Christ's presence does not stay in this one place. We learn to recognize his presence in the close circle in order to also recognize his presence elsewhere. As we also gather in neighborhoods "from house to house" (Acts 2:46) to eat, listen, exercise gifts, and be present to one another, so too Christ is present. This is the circle of discipleship because it happens amid day-to-day life where in his presence we can work out our salvation in fear and trembling.

We gather in neighborhoods just like Jesus did when he fed the five thousand (Mark 6:30-44). This dotted circle is still formed by a group of Christians in the neighborhood all committed to discerning his lordship (Mark 6:30), but there are gaps in this circle, places where people can see what God is doing (this is why I call it the dotted circle). Here, as we live everyday life, there are openings for outsiders to see what this Jesus is all about, how he rules, how he works. As Jesus works, heals, reconciles, and transforms our lives, people around us can see and be amazed. Here the Christian disciple hosts (Mark 6:37) as opposed to Jesus being the host in the first circle. Kingdom breaks out in the neighborhood and many are invited to join in as the Spirit moves.

*The half circle.* And yet Christ's presence is not exclusive to these places in the neighborhood either. He rules and is present over the whole world. And so the church moves out into social spaces among the broken, the hurting, the oppressed, the marginalized ("all the people" Acts 2:47). We go as Jesus went, not as a host but as a guest (Luke 19:7). We eat what is set before us (Luke 10:8). We sit among people, to listen to what God is doing among "the least of these" (Matthew 25:40). We are not in control.

In groups of no less than two, we are sent out (Luke 10:1). But in these places, we are actually "with" those who do not yet know him as Lord. I call this the half circle (or open circle) because the space is open. We who know him as Lord enter as guests and are with those who do not yet know his fullness. There is no question that Christ is present and at work in these places, but it is still (and must be) an open question as to whether he will be recognized.

When Christ's presence is revealed at work in the half circle, we who sit as guests humbly give witness to the good news. We listen and recognize someone in the process of being forgiven and healed. We gather over a conflict in town, a revealed injustice, or a grievous evil being rebuked. We see the conviction of the Spirit, an unselfish act, a physical healing, a reconciliation, or coalescence around reparative legislation. In all these we can proclaim, "I believe I see Jesus (as Lord) at work in this place! Can you see him too?" Strongholds are broken (Luke 10:17-19). Jesus manifests his presence. We invite those around into his kingdom. The town is transformed.

Each time someone recognizes his presence and receives his work, they too are added to this great kingdom coming. The church bears witness to and participates in the inbreaking of the new heaven and the new earth in every nook and cranny of our towns or villages. If the first circle was the worship place, and the second circle was the discipleship place, this half circle is the place of his mission.

## MAINTENANCE OR EXHAUSTION?

The church is not a set of programs offered at a central meeting place. It is a whole way of life lived in all three circles. This is the "how" of the church, and this "how" has everything to do with the "where" that the church takes shape—in all three places of life, not just one.

Often, when an existing church enters a crisis and the number of people gathering on Sunday in the close circle starts to shrink (along with weekly giving), pastors batten down the hatches and put all their focus on that first close circle. We work to keep the people who are showing up at the Sunday gathering (the close circle) coming. We do everything we can to keep everyone happy. Strangely, because we are comfortable preserving the church that gathers on Sundays only, we find ourselves defending our beliefs and what we do and why. We lose touch with those outside the church in the struggling places of pain in our neighborhoods. We turn inward on ourselves. We become introverted.

These are all signs that the church has moved into maintenance mode. It has moved away from church as a way of life that engages the world for God's mission. It cannot grow. It will surely die a slow death. And the pastor will look back after thirty or forty years of ministry, to that one time when all three hundred people were happy at the same time, and count it the highlight of his or her ministry.

But this is not what the church is. Maintenance mode is a sign that we must ask all over again the what, why, and how questions of the church, so that we too can once again be shaped into being the people of God in the greatest mission on earth.

In another vein, there are Christians and even pastors who are frustrated with the church's lack of engaging the world for God's justice. They have spent years of their life in a maintenance church that was overprotective, dispassionate toward a lost and broken world, rarely engaging the issues of a changing culture. They ask why we need the church at all to engage the world for Christ, his work for justice and transformation in the world. And they put their entire focus on the half circle to the exclusion of the other two circles.

What happens here is that such a church loses the wherewithal to discern, trust, and participate in Jesus' living presence among the hurting, oppressed, and broken places of the world. Without a deep sense of his presence learned in the close circle, Christians forget how Jesus is present in the open circles of our lives. We soon rely on human effort to accomplish what we believe is God's justice in the world.

In a matter of years, if not months, when money and human resources get stretched, we will be exhausted. We end up accomplishing a few things via human effort because God can use even human effort. But the world is not transformed. Eventually, when our own energy runs out and we ourselves must exit, the work grinds to a halt. It is revealed that this was human work, not the work empowered by the risen Christ.

There are of course churches that have sought to focus singularly on the middle circles of discipleship to the exclusion of the other two circles. This too results in a lopsided church.

These churches often become cliques of various kinds, focusing either on friendship and becoming enclosed or on a social cause. They last only as long as the interest in that cause can be sustained.

These examples illustrate that it is absolutely imperative, whatever our proclivities, to organize the church as a whole way of life, in all three circles of life. We may start in any one of the three circles, but the church eventually must become present in all three circles of our lives.

## RECOVERING THE CHURCH

Members of the New Testament church, as best we can tell, lived the practices in all three circles of their lives.[3] They ate the Lord's table together and discerned his presence at the close circle gathering, what became the institutional eucharist celebration. But they also ate together and discerned his presence around tables in their homes. They shared food and beverage with the hurting and marginalized peoples among them. The Lord's table was practiced in all three circles. All the practices were cultivated in these three circles the first two hundred years of church life, as shown in the New Testament.[4]

But as Christianity spread, when the Roman Empire sponsored Christianity as the accepted religion of the state, millions of people converted to Christianity and the church had to organize efficiently. It is here that we see the beginning of the centralization of church organization. The practices given by Christ to the disciples for all of life were organized into one central place and a priest was put in charge of their proper administration. Where once Christians had practiced his presence at all the tables where they ate, the focus was now put on Sunday morning.[5] Where once Christians would pray and anoint for healing everywhere, including in the streets, now the prayer of healing was conducted by a priest in a church cathedral. Indeed, the practices once experienced in all of life became centralized in the close circle gathering of the church.

We should not be too stern in judgment on the emerging Roman Catholic Church of the fourth century and beyond. They had a mammoth task. Millions of new Christians were flowing into the church and they had to organize swiftly and efficiently.

But today we face a different situation. We no longer have masses of people flowing into our church. We have masses leaving it. We no longer live in a Christendom-based culture tasked with organizing Christians. We are a post-Christendom church tasked with organizing Christians into the mission of God in the world. Our call is different: We must recover the three circles of the New Testament church. We must extend the practices from the one centralized gathering into all the circles of life. We must recultivate the practices, not to happen in one place but as practices cultivated in all three places of our lives. This is the task before us.

# Epilogue

As the sun sets on Christendom in the West and churches everywhere face disruption and decline, the questions stir among us. Will we be faithful to the call of Jesus to be his church in North America? Will we set about asking the what, why, and how questions of the church all over again?

## THE WAY GOD CHANGES THE WORLD

I have answered the "what" question with the practices that shape a practicing community in Jesus. To answer the "why" question I have described how presence, as the way God works, requires a people and relationships for God to be present among and through to change the world. In addressing the "how" question, I have showed how the church must be organized in three places for it truly to be the church in mission. These three Ps—Practices, Presence, and Places—I suggest can provide a foundation for leading our churches to renewal. Will we lead our churches through a recommitment to the core practices of our lives together, a deepening experience of the living presence of the risen Lord in all of life, and a reconnection to being the church in all three places of our lives?

Surely many more questions remain. How do we get an overly comfortable, defensive, protective, or even presumptuous church to ask the what, why, and how questions? How do we lead the reorganization of a church into three circles when we have been stuck in centralized mode for so long? For many, the task of leading a church into renewal (or planting a church like this) seems daunting.

Let us take a deep breath and recognize that this task is not up to us. The task of renewing Christ's church is his work. Let us pray, discern, and find ways to be patient in cultivating the social spaces for Jesus to manifest his presence among us.

Let us start small. Instead of reorganizing an entire church into three circles, begin with twelve people eating dinner on a regular evening in someone's home. Instead of launching a new church with ten thousand postcards and a gala event, start with finding twelve people to gather regularly for a meal in your neighborhood. As you eat, invoke his presence. Listen to one another. Tend to the presence of Christ at a meal. Patiently work out your lives together in fear and trembling. Engage in the practices. Pray for your neighbors, for the issues in the neighborhood. Submit all things to Christ's rule in prayer. Allow God to work in these smallest of gatherings to heal bodies, save marriages, bring down racist strongholds in the village. Then let it spread. Organize in all three circles of life.

Let us ask questions of one another about where God is calling us into mission and share the vision for God's kingdom coming to this place. Ask people if they are interested in being a part of Christ's kingdom here in this town. Help them find their half circle or dotted circle. Teach them how to be present there, and discern his presence, practice reconciliation, and, when the time is right, proclaim the good news of Jesus and all the practices of Christ's presence. I call these "kingdom cups of coffee."

When the bigger gathering happens, often on Sundays, let us gather to tell stories of wonder from where God was at work this past week. Teach the whats, the whys and the hows of what God in Christ is calling us into. But realize that, for most people, it will be when people see and hear of God working that they too will join in. God always seems to start out small, doing great and mighty things in unsuspecting ways in people's lives for all to see. It is from this that people will be drawn into God's kingdom. It is from this that people shall be saved. It is the way God changes the world.

I have a famous friend, who leads a church that has had a mammoth impact in his community over forty-plus years. People now come from all around the world to see what God has done. He once told me, "Dave, if you would have been here after fifteen years of ministry, you would have said nothing is happening here." And yet the seeds were being planted, plants were taking root, slowly people's lives were being changed, until the tide turned, and a whole neighborhood of many thousands of people was changed some years later. This is the way God changes the world.

And so, "Let us not grow weary in doing what is right, for we will reap at harvest time, if we do not give up" (Galatians 6:9). Let us seek a new faithfulness in cultivating Christ's church as a whole way of life in all the towns, villages, boroughs, and neighborhoods of the world. Let God's kingdom infest our country until the completion of the age.

# Glossary

**Christendom:** Refers to a society where the majority culture is assumed to be Christian, where the church assumes that the culture and state will align with the church and its Christian values and purposes. The medieval period in Europe is the archetypal example of a Christendom culture where the church and state aligned to order society.

**Constantinian:** Describes the character of the fourth-century Roman social world, where the Emperor Constantine used the power of the state to sponsor, support, and even organize the Christian church. The adjective also refers to any time the church relies unduly on state or cultural resources and authority to exert influence in society.

***ekklesia:*** A Greek word used to describe the church in the New Testament.

**manifest presence:** Though God is present everywhere (omnipresence), God becomes manifestly present when God becomes present in concrete, visceral ways among people—in ways that can be seen, felt, and encountered.

**Nicene Creed:** A statement of belief widely used in worship in Christian churches around the world. It is called Nicene because it was originally adopted in the city of Nicaea by the First Council of Nicaea in 325.

**omnipresence:** Refers to the fact that God is present everywhere at once, all the time. In the words of A.W. Tozer, God is "everywhere here, close to everything, next to everyone." (*Knowledge of the Holy,* Harrisburg, PA: Christian Publications, 1961, 57).

**practice:** An exercise done repeatedly together as a people to allow a particular goal or purpose to be achieved in our midst. As opposed to an idea—a practice embodies the idea in something we do.

**triune God:** Though God is one, God is three persons—Father, Son, and Holy Spirit. It is the nature of God that his work in the world is triune, in which the Father sends the Son into the world, and the Spirit processes from the Son and the Father, and the church is caught up into his mission, the triune movement of God into the world.

**sacrament:** In the Roman Catholic tradition, a sacrament is an outward sign instituted by Christ to minister his grace into the lives of believers. Sacraments are practices we do with material realities (like water, bread, wine, food, oil) wherein God promises to be present and work.

**social sacrament:** This phrase, used by Anabaptist theologian John Howard Yoder, refers to certain prescribed social activities wherein Christ promises to become especially present "in and with, through and under what men and women do" together in social spaces.

# Discussion and Reflection Questions

## CHAPTER 1

1. Where does your local church put more emphasis, on practices or beliefs? Give examples.
2. Which New Testament names, Nicene Creedal names, or descriptions for the church do you most resonate with as a description of your own church, church as you've known it, or the church as you long for it to be?
3. When a belief is challenged in your church, how does your church lead to resolution? How does your church do hierarchical authority, practices of conversation, discernment, or prayer?

## CHAPTER 2

1. How do belief statements work in the life of your church? Who pays attention to them? What role do practices play in organizing your church?
2. Is your church organized primarily through programs at a centralized location? Or as practices carried out in various places of ministry outside the church building?
3. Do you see your church as defensive or engaging when beliefs or practices of the church are questioned? Does you church invite questioning?
4. Which of the core practices listed in the chapter drive the life of your church? Is your church missing any practices?

## CHAPTER 3

1. Why do you participate (or not participate) in a church? Do you see church as essential for making space for God to work through his presence?
2. "It is by God's presence that God works." How does this sentence shape your imagination for God working in your life, your church, your neighborhood?
3. Have you experienced a sense of God's presence at work in you? In your church? Around you? In others? Describe what you experienced.

## CHAPTER 4

1. When you hear the words "kingdom of God," when you think of Jesus being a king ruling over the world, what negative or positive images come to your imagination?
2. If we learn that it is by God's presence, not coercion, that God rules in and through Jesus, (what Don

Kraybill calls "the upside-down kingdom"), how does this change your understanding and participation in God's kingdom?

3.  If mission is not a program of our local church, but it is God's mission, by God's presence, into which we are invited to participate, how does this change your attitude or posture as you enter the world's injustice or brokenness?

## CHAPTER 5

1.  Do you experience the practice of the Lord's table as a personal discipline for your own personal growth, or as social space where Christ is at work among a group of people? Describe how this works in your church.

2.  Is your church organized to gather people in a central place? Or in dispersed places over your geographical region? Why do you think your church organizes the way it does?

3.  What social spaces have the most impact in your life? Where are they? Are they connected to your church? Why are they so impactful?

## CHAPTER 6

1.  Of the three circles, is there a circle that your church emphasizes over the other two? Why do you think that is?

2.  Which malady seems to plague your church or your group of Christian friends, maintenance church or exhaustion church? Why? What are the signs?

3.  What are the biggest challenges to your church cultivating the social spaces in all three circles of our lives?

# Shared Convictions

*Mennonite World Conference, a global community of Christian churches that facilitates community between Anabaptist-related churches, offers these shared convictions that characterize Anabaptist faith. For more on Anabaptism, go to ThirdWayCafe.com.*

By the grace of God, we seek to live and proclaim the good news of reconciliation in Jesus Christ. As part of the one body of Christ at all times and places, we hold the following to be central to our belief and practice:

1. God is known to us as Father, Son and Holy Spirit, the Creator who seeks to restore fallen humanity by calling a people to be faithful in fellowship, worship, service and witness.

2. Jesus is the Son of God. Through his life and teachings, his cross and resurrection, he showed us how to be faithful disciples, redeemed the world, and offers eternal life.

3.  As a church, we are a community of those whom God's Spirit calls to turn from sin, acknowledge Jesus Christ as Lord, receive baptism upon confession of faith, and follow Christ in life.

4.  As a faith community, we accept the Bible as our authority for faith and life, interpreting it together under Holy Spirit guidance, in the light of Jesus Christ to discern God's will for our obedience.

5.  The Spirit of Jesus empowers us to trust God in all areas of life so we become peacemakers who renounce violence, love our enemies, seek justice, and share our possessions with those in need.

6.  We gather regularly to worship, to celebrate the Lord's Supper, and to hear the Word of God in a spirit of mutual accountability.

7.  As a world-wide community of faith and life we transcend boundaries of nationality, race, class, gender and language. We seek to live in the world without conforming to the powers of evil, witnessing to God's grace by serving others, caring for creation, and inviting all people to know Jesus Christ as Saviour and Lord.

In these convictions we draw inspiration from Anabaptist forebears of the 16th century, who modelled radical discipleship to Jesus Christ. We seek to walk in his name by the power of the Holy Spirit, as we confidently await Christ's return and the final fulfillment of God's kingdom.

*Adopted by Mennonite World Conference General Council, March 15, 2006*

# Notes

## Chapter 1

1 For the meaning of the Greek word *ekklesia* in Greco-Roman and Jewish contexts, see *The Oxford Illustrated History of Greece and the Hellenistic World* (Cambridge: Oxford University Press, 2001), 130–36; L. Coenen, "Church," in *New International Dictionary of New Testament Theology*, ed. Colin Brown (Grand Rapids: Zondervan, 1986), 1:291. For an expansive treatment of the subject, see Young-Ho Park, *Paul's Ekklesia as a Civic Assembly* (Tubingen: Mohr Siebeck, 2014).

2 In the words of Anabaptist theologian John Howard Yoder, the church "has ways of making decisions, defining membership, and carrying out common tasks." *Body Politics: Five Practices of the Christian Community before the Watching World* (Scottdale, PA: Herald Press, 1992), viii. I quote Yoder with discernment, recognizing his personal history of abuse toward women within his orbit of influence while a professor at Associated Mennonite Biblical Seminary in Elkhart, Ind., and at the University of Notre Dame. For a treatment of the problem of quoting Yoder that I am sympathetic with, please read Lisa Schirch, "Afterword: To the Next Generation of Pacifist Theologians," in *John Howard Yoder: Radical Theologian*, ed. J. Denny Weaver (Eugene, OR: Cascade Books, 2014), 377–95.

3  For liturgical and other reasons, the original creed's "We believe"
   was eventually translated (into Latin) for use in the Roman
   Catholic mass as "I believe."

4  Ephraim Radner, *A Brutal Unity* (Waco, TX: Baylor University
   Press, 2012).

5  This is not to suggest that what the church believes is always up
   for negotiation. Quite the contrary. The Nicene Creed settled some
   markers as to what the church believes. That Jesus is fully God
   and fully human was established at Nicaea, where the Council of
   Nicaea interpreted what that means for the Greco-Roman world
   of 313–383 AD. But of course this belief must be extended into the
   rest of the world and must be interpreted for every culture. A Greco-Roman interpretation from a particular time and culture cannot
   unilaterally be forced onto all the rest of the world's cultures,
   where perhaps a Greco-Roman metaphysics makes little or no
   sense. For this reason, the practice of allowing the Spirit to extend,
   rather than enforce, faithfulness into all the world requires that
   we allow disagreement, and that we make space for the practice
   of dialogue and reconciliation in the midst of disagreements under
   the reign of Jesus. This is what unity means for the church in all
   times and all places. For a treatment of this subject, see Alain Epp
   Weaver, "Missionary Christology: John Howard Yoder and the
   Creeds," *Mennonite Quarterly Review*, 74 (3), 423–440, 2000.

6  Interestingly, Anabaptists have traditionally criticized the second
   article of the historic creeds for focusing intently on Christ's
   divinity and humanity and the accomplished work of Christ on the
   cross and the resurrection, but saying little about the significance
   of his actual life. The focus on the nature and relationship of his
   divinity and humanity overwhelmed his life and the themes so
   central for discipleship. See Epp Weaver, "Missionary Christology"
   437, and Thomas Finger, *A Contemporary Anabaptist Theology:
   Biblical, Historical, Constructive* (Downers Grove, IL: IVP
   Academic, 2010), 109.

7  To be sure there was still a practice involved here—ordination
   and consecration of priests. But this practice now becomes more
   positional and authority becomes less associated with the communal participation of the gifts and more aligned with the hierarchical
   function of office.

8  This account of the clash between the Anabaptists and Luther
   is dependent on John Howard Yoder's historical account of the

*notae missionis* (marks of mission) in John Howard Yoder, *Royal Priesthood* (Scottdale, PA: Herald Press, 1998), 75–89.

## Chapter 2

1  In *The End of Evangelicalism?* (Eugene, OR: Cascade Books, 2011), xv–xvii, and indeed throughout the book, I argue that beliefs plus practices shape a culture. Both beliefs and practices, working together, are necessary to shape a whole way of life.

2  Because in each practice, what we believe is lived. For instance, the way Jesus' person and work is connected to his death, his forgiveness, and his presence is woven into the practice of the table. The belief that in Christ we are forgiven and we forgive is lived in the practice of reconciliation. Doctrine is both interwoven and lived in each practice. Leaders can only lead us in the practices by also teaching all the beliefs that drive them.

3  In my *The Church of Us vs.Them* I argue this at length, that when beliefs are extracted from practices, they turn into banners that shape a people to be against an object, and actually detach a people from living out the belief in everyday life. See *The Church of Us vs. Them* (Grand Rapids, MI: Brazos Press, 2019), ch. 2.

4  This principle is played out in church planting practices as well. Starting churches in a Christendom context, for example, often starts with a website describing the new church's services and belief statements. This only makes sense in Christendom, as the only people interested in a church's belief statement before they come to a church are already existing Christians. When we start churches with belief statements, we are in essence admitting that we are planting this church to attract already existing Christians with a better form of church. On the other hand, if a church plant starts by defining its foundational practices, and inviting other Christians to come along with them and inhabit a particular place for Jesus' reign, this church is seeking primarily to give witness to the gospel of God's Kingdom in this place. This kind of starting church needs assume no preexisting Christendom (or refuses to organize on its terms) and hence starts with practices.

5  This can be found in great detail in David E. Fitch, *Faithful Presence: Seven Disciplines that Shape the Church for Mission* (Downers Grove, IL: IVP Books, 2016).

6  Roman Catholic historian Joseph Martos noted that twelfth century lists of Roman Catholic sacraments ranged from twelve

to thirty. *Doors to the Sacred* (Ligouri, MO: Ligouri/Triumph, 2001), 50.

7 For a full treatment of the practices, see Fitch, *Faithful Presence*.

## Chapter 3

1 This quote is from John Walton, *The Lost World of Genesis One* (Downers Grove, IL: IVP Academic, 2009), 83.

2 G.K. Beale argues that the Genesis account of the garden of Eden portrays Eden as the first sanctuary, a recapitulation of the first temple. *The Temple and the Church's Mission* (Downers Grove, IL: IVP Books, 2004), 66–80. See also Jon D. Levenson, *Sinai and Zion: An Entry Into The Jewish Bible* (New York: Harper-One, 1987).

3 This history is expounded in my *Faithful Presence: Seven Disciplines that Shape the Church for Mission* (Downers Grove, IL: IVP Books, 2016), ch. 1.

4 Of course one significant objection to this account of God's presence and the way he works in the Old Testament is the apparent holy wars of Israel, the genocide and killing often at the direction, wrath, and judgment of God. I have space here to only say is that I do not subscribe to this interpretation. In this regard I have found helpful Gregory Boyd, *Crucifixion of the Warrior God*, Vols. 1 & 2 (Minneapolis: Fortress Press, 2017), and John Nugent, *Politics of Yahweh* (Eugene, OR: Cascade Books, 2011) .

5 Beale, *The Temple*, ch. 1, ch. 12.

6 Large parts of this section were borrowed and adapted from *Faithful Presence*, 21–24.

## Chapter 4

1 Perhaps a good place to start is N.T. Wright, *Jesus and the Victory of God* (Minneapolis: Fortress Press, 1997).

2 This narrative concerning the monarchy of Israel was outlined by John Howard Yoder. See John Nugent, *Politics of Yahweh* (Eugene OR: Cascade Books, 2011), ch. 4 for a summary of it.

3 See Donald Kraybill's classic on this theme, *The Upside-Down Kingdom* (Harrisonburg, VA: Herald Press, 1978).

4 Walter Rauschenbusch, *A Theology for the Social Gospel* (New York: MacMillan Company, 1917), ch. 8.

5 See Scot McKnight, *Kingdom Conspiracy: A Return to the Radical Mission of the Local Church* (Grand Rapids, MI: Brazos Press,

2014) for a treatment of the biblical understanding of the relationship between the kingdom of God and the church.

6 Jürgen Moltmann, *The Church in the Power of the Spirit* (New York: Harper & Row, 1977), 64.

7 A complete exposition on Ephesians 1:23 as a political theology for the church's engagement with the world can be found in David E. Fitch, *The Church of Us vs. Them* (Grand Rapids: Brazos Press, 2019), Appendix I, 173–181.

8 Markus Barth makes this case (while also referring to other scholars) in *Ephesians: Introduction* (New York: Doubleday, 1974), 203–205.

9 A symbolic text in this regard is the description of God's presence in Isaiah 6:1-3. "The Lord sitting upon a throne . . . his train filled the temple" (RSV). And yet also in the same text, the seraphim testified that "the whole earth is full of his glory."

10 There is an extended treatment of the twofold movement of the Son in *Faithful Presence*. I describe this principle as "missio Dei + incarnation = witness." See Appendix 3 of *Faithful Presence* (Downers Grove, IL: IVP Books, 2016), 197–205. In seeing the church as the extension of Christ's manifest presence, it is important to recognize the asymmetrical relationship between the church and Jesus. The church is totally dependent on Jesus for his presence among us, for its every existence. Jesus however is not dependent on the church in any way for his existence. Barth explains this relationship via the Chalcedonian terms *enhypostasis* and *anhypostasis*. See *Faithful Presence*, 202 and 227, note 17.

11 The church does not control Jesus' presence. Rather, as the church submits to his lordship, it opens space for his presence (omnipresence) to become visible (manifest presence). His kingdom breaks in. Mighty works take place. The world sees Jesus, where he is taking the whole world, and all are invited to join in and be part of his kingdom. Jesus' omnipresent reign takes on flesh manifestly throughout the world via the church. This is the answer to the "why" church question.

12 *Faithful Presence*, 10.

## Chapter 5

1 The Roman Catholics believe this happens at *the words of institution* while the Eastern Orthodox see this happening at the prayer of epiclesis.

2 John Howard Yoder is an important theologian to my work. To reiterate however, I quote him carefully, recognizing that Yoder was found guilty of abusive sexual behavior in his past, and his work must be judged and discerned carefully and accordingly.

3 John Howard Yoder, *Body Politics: Five Practices of the Christian Community Before the Watching World* (Scottdale, PA: Herald Press, 2001), 71–73.

## Chapter 6

1 I have devoted considerable space in *Faithful Presence* (Downers Grove, IL: IVP Books, 2016) to show how with each practice, there is New Testament evidence that it took place in all three spaces of the Christian life, what I call the three circles.

2 You can find the three circles described in detail in *Faithful Presence*, 40–43.

3 I have developed these three circle concepts over years of study and ministry. Nonetheless, the idea of three places for the church practices is not without precedent. Andrew B. McGowan, for instance, describes different settings for eating around the table in the first centuries of the church. See Hippolytus, *The Apostolic Tradition*, and McGowan, *Ancient Christian Worship* (Grand Rapids: Baker Academic, 2014), 50–51. Russell E. Riche sees three different meal settings in some streams of Methodism: "Family Meal, Holy Communion, and Love Feasts: Three Ecumenical Metaphors," in *Ecumenical and Interreligious Perspectives* (Nashville: Quarterly Review of Books, 1992), 17–29.

4 I have built this case throughout my book *Faithful Presence*.

5 In the *Didache*'s instructions for the eucharist, 10.1 speaks of just having completed a full meal, while 10.6 invites people to receive communion after the meal. Evidently there were two kinds of meals practiced and related to each other. The eucharist was practiced in various ways around meals and in homes as well as more formal church gatherings. Paul Bradshaw argues that by the time of the Peace of Constantine, the meals had been largely unified into a single practice under the priest. For many reasons, not the least of which was the "desire to curb a practice that was not subject to ecclesiastical control (to not allow Arians to receive communion) the Council of Saragossa (379–81) and Toledo (400)" tried to prevent the sacrament from being taken home. Paul Bradshaw, *Reconstructing Early Christian Worship* (Collegeville, MN: Liturgical Press, 2009), 37. See further ch. 2–3.

# The Author

**D**avid E. Fitch is B. R. Lindner Chair of Evangelical Theology at Northern Seminary, Chicago, Illinois. He is also one of the cofounders of Missio Alliance. He is the founding pastor of Life on the Vine Christian Community, a missional church in the northwest suburbs of Chicago, and part of the pastoral staff of a daughter congregation, Peace of Christ Church in Westmont, Illinois. He writes on the issues the local church must face in mission, including cultural engagement, leadership, and theology, and has lectured and presented on these topics at many seminaries, graduate schools, denominational gatherings, and conferences. His books include *The Church of Us vs. Them* and *Faithful Presence: Seven Disciplines that Shape the Church for Mission*.

## SMALL BOOKS

# THE JESUS WAY

### of RADICAL FAITH

**What Is the Bible and How Do We Understand It?**
*by Dennis R. Edwards*

**Why Did Jesus Die and What Difference Does It Make?**
*by Michele Hershberger*

**What Is the Trinity and Why Does It Matter?**
*by Steve Dancause*

**Why Do We Suffer and Where Is God When We Do?**
*by Valerie G. Rempel*

**Who Are Our Enemies and How Do We Love Them?**
*by Hyung Jin Kim Sun*

**What Does Justice Look Like and Why Does God Care about It?**
*by Judith and Colin McCartney*

**What Is God's Mission in the World and How Do We Join It?**
*by Juan Francisco Martinez and Jamie Pitts*

**What Is the Church and Why Does It Exist?**
*by David E. Fitch*

**What Is God's Kingdom and What Does Citizenship Look Like?**
*by César García*

**Who Was Jesus and What Does It Mean to Follow Him?**
*by Nancy Elizabeth Bedford*

# HERALD
### PRESS

www.HeraldPress.com. 1-800-245-7894